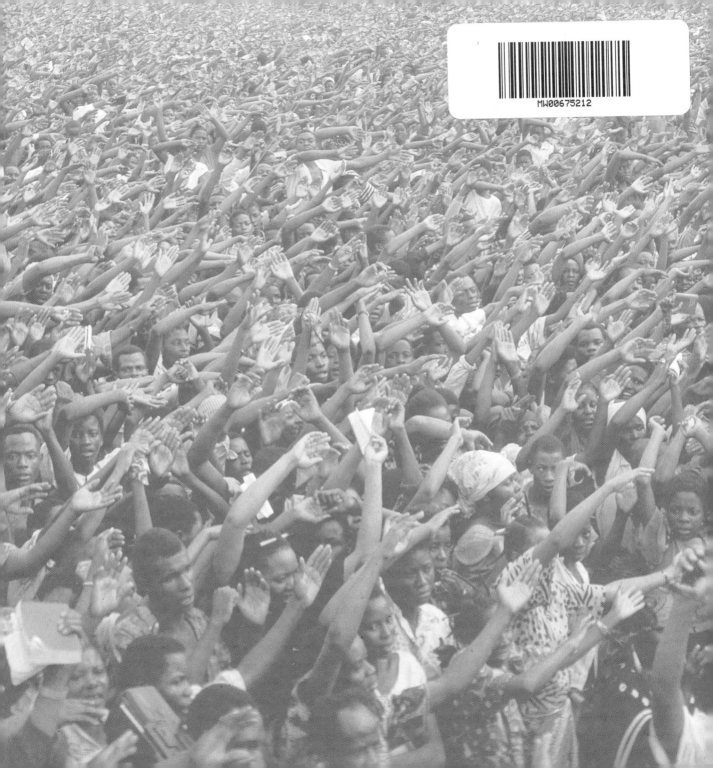

Reinhard Bonnke:
The Boy Whose Life Touched Millions

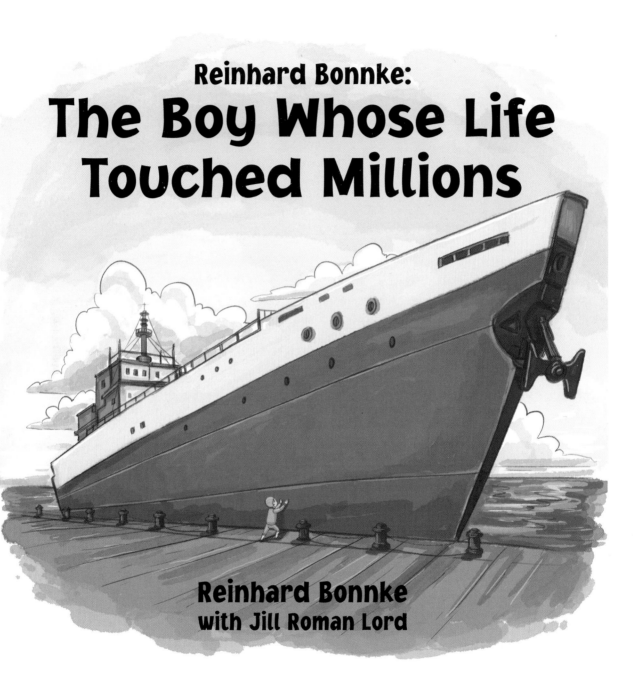

Reinhard Bonnke
with Jill Roman Lord

Introduction

What do a circus, a ship, and a dance hall for teens all have in common? God used events at all those places to help form me into the person He could use to bring millions of people to know our Lord and Savior, Jesus Christ.

I am Reinhard Bonnke.

I'd like to share these true stories of my life with you.

*H*onk, *Splash, Bam!* Those are sounds I heard as a 5-year-old boy escaping from Germany during World War II with my mother and siblings squeezed onto a ship with many others. My father would meet up with us later. The ship's horn *honked* as we headed to the safety of Copenhagen, Denmark. Once at sea, the ship bounced and *splashed* and swayed back and forth. Have you ever been on a rocking boat? It made many of us sick. In the middle of the night we got hit with a sea mine *Bam!* and water rushed in. I was so scared. The boat began to lean to one side. Men worked hard to pump out the water. I thought we'd sink for sure.

Mother called us to her side and prayed reminding us that God could make a path in the mighty waters. Soon the ship began to straighten itself. Whew! At last we arrived at Copenhagen. I felt like Mother had prayed us to safety the whole way. Deep inside my heart, I wanted to know this God the way she knew Him.

When I was ten years old in 1950, one Sunday in church, I felt the Lord speak His words into my heart, "Reinhard, one day you will preach my gospel in Africa." I didn't even know where Africa was. But I knew that is where I needed to be some day, and this excited me.

My father had also heard God speak to his heart and became a pastor after the war, preaching in his own small church. I knew he would be so happy to hear my word from God. But he was not. Even when a woman at a prayer meeting shared that I was the one in her vision sharing bread with a growing crowd of black people, my Father did not believe me. He wanted my oldest brother to become a preacher, not me. This made me very sad. However, I liked this woman's encouragement of my purpose from God and I carried this in my heart.

Later that year, I went to the grocery store with my mother. I noticed a colorful poster in the window about a circus coming to town. The world seemed dark and boring following the war and there weren't many colorful things or fun sites around, so this poster really captured my attention. I begged my mother to let me stay outside.

While she shopped, I studied this fascinating poster and memorized the date that the train would roll into town. It showed African lions jumping through hoops, horses, bears, monkeys, and an elephant that would help put up the poles for the tent! Wow!

Have you ever been to the circus? I wanted to see that. But when Mother returned she expressed her disappointment in me. While I explained my fascination with the animals, she said the circus was a worldly event and she worried that my heart was being led astray. She stuffed the grocery bags into my arms and warned me not to go near that place. I helped carry the groceries home with my mind still focused on the circus.

The day the circus train rolled into town, I snuck away to see it. I just had to! I saw the tigers, lions and bears in their cages on the train. I walked along the tracks looking at each of the exotic animals. This filled me with such wonder!

The animal trainers used the horses and elephants to haul the big tent from the train to the field. I followed them the whole way. I loved watching the elephant push the huge tent pole into place in the center of the field. This truly amazed me. I stayed and watched it all.

Have you ever disobeyed your parents? When I got home, I found myself in a lot of trouble. A friend of Mother's had seen me watching the tent being put up and told her. She was really upset that I disobeyed her, and I got the 'time-out' of my life. I felt very bad for disappointing her. I felt like I let her down and let God down. I learned the importance of obedience.

next to last. That was my position in the family - a position that was easily overlooked. My oldest brother was Martin, whom my father wanted to become a preacher. Next was Gerhard who was very athletic. Then came a set of twins, Juergen and Peter, and behind me was the only daughter, Felicitas, the apple of her daddy's eye. I seemed to always get in trouble, but felt like my calling from God to go to Africa gave purpose to my unremarkable life.

now back in Germany, we enrolled in school and found that we were all behind the other German students. My older brothers caught up quickly. I did not. All classes were hard for me, but I really did not like English. It was so different from the German that I spoke. I could not learn the rules of that crazy language. My brothers could, and they tormented me. I felt like a failure compared to them.

We lived close to the water and I liked to get away from my teasing brothers and come to the pier on the Elbe River to dream. I longed to be aboard a boat and sail away to Africa to fulfill my calling.

One day a large ship sat by the pier and I remembered our desperate journey to Copenhagen. I reached out from the dock and touched it! I touched it again, pushed with all my might and moved the ship a few inches from the pier. Can you believe it? I actually moved that massive boat! On shore it would have been impossible to move, but on water it was possible, even for me, a twelve-year-old boy. God spoke to my heart - when He asks me to do the impossible, I should obey. His ways are limitless, and nothing is impossible with God.

When I grew up. I attended an English-speaking bible college in Wales, then felt God calling me to Flensburg, Germany as I could not go to Africa yet. I did not know anybody there and did not have a church of my own, so I set up a little tent in a field for six weeks at a time and preached the gospel, the good news about Jesus Christ.

The first night, an old farmer came forward to accept Jesus as his Savior. More and more people came each night. Halfway through my first six weeks, fifty people had come to know the Lord. This was exciting for me!

Then a circus came to town and set up next to us in the same field! That huge circus tent towered over my tiny little tent. I felt like everybody would go to the big circus and not come to hear about God.

One day, the circus director popped into my little tent and asked me to preach in his big tent! I couldn't believe it. "Preach to the circus crowd?" Yes! He would advertise, and I could preach to a tent full of people who needed to know about Jesus.

As I walked through the tent that Sunday morning, with the tall tent poles holding the large tent, I prayed to God for a circus-sized tent where people would come - not to see a circus - but to expect to meet Jesus there.

I preached and had an altar call - that's when I ask who wants to receive Jesus as their Savior, forgiveness for their sins and to enter God's plan for their lives. Those who are willing, raise their hands. I heard weeping behind me. It was the circus clown sobbing and shaking from head to toe. He knelt before me, wanting to receive Jesus as His Savior. I led him in the prayer of salvation - in giving his heart to Jesus. He finished his circus performances, then quit the circus and joined my congregation!

Soon after that, I married the love of my heart, Anni, and we finally moved to Africa. This made me so happy! I preached on street corners of Lesotho, a country in Southern Africa. I played my accordion and sang to bring in the crowds, then I'd preach the gospel. My congregation grew to fifty people!

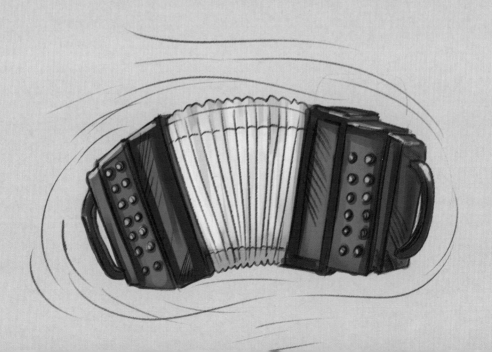

My friend Harold asked me to speak one weekend at a church in a town known for its diamond mines. The world's largest diamonds came from this town! I spoke Friday night and was pleased that 200 people came, but only old people had come. I like old people, but wondered where the younger kids were. Harold took me to where the young people hung out...

A disco! Do you know what a disco is? I did not. But I learned. BOOM! BOOM! BOOM! The ground shook beneath us with the blast of head-banging music, as we stood outside. This was a place where kids danced! I was afraid and every part of me wanted to leave. But I felt God tugging on my heart to enter and I would obey, though I had no idea what I would do once inside. I wondered what the kids could possibly find there that they needed.

So, Harold and I entered the deafening light-flashing disco, found the owner and asked if I could have five minutes with this group. He figured out that I must be a preacher and told me to preach in a church. I explained that the young people did not go to church, they came to discos. Would you believe that he agreed to give me five minutes with them at midnight the next evening? It's true! I was so excited I could have kissed him!

I kicked myself for only asking for five minutes. Then I thought, God created the world in six days and would have no problem saving a disco in five minutes! I knew with God nothing was too hard.

I preached to the old people the next night, then Harold and I changed into our "dancing" clothes and arrived at the disco just before midnight.

When the clock struck 12:00, the music stopped, and I jumped onto the stage. I told everyone to sit down because I was from Germany and had something important to tell them. They plopped on the floor. I started preaching and felt the wind of God blow into that disco. People began crying, and I mean sobbing! When I offered an altar call, everyone's hands went up. We prayed the prayer of salvation together and my five minutes were up. I rejoiced that I could help them find in a disco what they could never find otherwise - Jesus.

During my next visit, a year later, Harold had a surprise for me. He drove me to the disco, but instead it had become a church! That place was packed! Many asked me if I remembered them. They had been the ones playing the music and operating the lights. Others said they had been dancing but now they were serving Jesus. These kids in the diamond town had now become precious gems of Christ their Savior.

After many years, I flew into South Africa from my travels and Anni picked me up. As we drove, I saw six large cranes around a huge structure. Tears rolled down my face as I realized this was a part of our big tent. We had been holding our meetings in tents, but they never had been big enough to hold the people the Lord brought to us. Now the Lord provided the biggest tent that had ever been made, and it looked enormous! People would come expecting to meet Jesus here.

News of the largest tent spread around the world and even to America! We didn't have stallions and elephants to haul our tent, but people generously donated to help purchase trucks to lug this tent over the rough roads in Africa. In the first meetings in that tent, we saw more than 25,000 decisions for Christ.

next, we set up this massive tent in Cape Town, Valhalla Park, which was known as the "Kill me Quick" area because many crimes occurred there. We increased our security so as not to lose any lives.

One afternoon, a whoosh of wind and pounding rain ripped the tent. The wind strengthened throughout the night and violently attacked our tent. By morning, only a few strands of fabric remained. The largest tent in the world, which took five years to create, was destroyed in five hours. How could we go on preaching to so many people without this tent?

People who disapproved of the size of the tent, thought it was a waste of money. To some this was a complete failure. My co-workers lost heart.

But, a pastor spoke a prophecy, or insight from God, to us, "My glory shall be the canopy that covers the people, and the praises of My people shall be the pillars." Maybe we didn't need a tent after all. Encouraged by these words, we agreed to continue with the meeting. But this was rainy season. Would another storm come? Would this be a complete disaster?

God held off the rain for a full three weeks! Because the largest tent in the world had been destroyed, people heard about us and came to see for themselves. Media spread news of our story. Believers and not-yet-believers came in crowds to hear the gospel. Our first meeting drew 25,000 people. Our final night, 75,000 attended. It became obvious that the world's largest tent would never have been big enough to hold the mass of people God planned to attract to Cape Town. During this meeting, not a single crime was reported, but criminals tossed their weapons onto the stage in repentance.

Conclusion

My Father admitted he was proud of me and that he was wrong in not believing God's call on my life as a ten-year-old boy. He even came to hear me preach. The circus, the ship and the disco, all served to remind me of the importance of obeying my parents and of obeying God. Though I was disobedient at times and felt like a failure at other times, God used me to lead multiplied millions upon millions of people to accept Jesus as their Savior. If He can use somebody like me, He can use somebody like you. Just receive Him as your Savior, open your heart to His leading and do your best to obey. Remember the ship I pushed? You can do the same. With God nothing is impossible.

Photo Album

1. My mother and her 6 children in the refugee camp in Denmark.

2. Myself on the left with my twin brothers

3. I am preaching in the small tent which seated 10,000 people

4. The large tent which seated 34,000 people in South Africa.

5. I am preaching the Gospel in Africa just like God had promised.

6. God allowed me to preach to 1,600,000 people in Lagos, Nigeria.

© 2019 by Reinhard Bonnke
REINHARD BONNKE: THE BOY WHOSE LIFE TOUCHED MILLIONS

Published by Christ for all Nations
PO Box 590588
Orlando, FL 32859-0588
CfaN.org

ISBN: 978-1-933446-78-3   Hardcover

Written by Reinhard Bonnke with Jill Roman Lord
Source Life Stories taken from LIVING A LIFE OF FIRE, An Autobiography by Reinhard Bonnke © 2010 Harvester Services, Inc.

Interior Design by Grupo Nivel Uno Inc.

Illustrations by Mi Victoria Designs, Havana, Cuba

International Rights managed by Harvester Services, Inc.

Printed in Colombia